Battle Flag Comittee

Report of the Battle Flag Committee

Appointed by the Twenty-Fourth General Assembly...

Battle Flag Comittee

Report of the Battle Flag Committee
Appointed by the Twenty-Fourth General Assembly...

ISBN/EAN: 9783744653664

Printed in Europe, USA, Canada, Australia, Japan

Cover: Foto ©ninafisch / pixelio.de

More available books at **www.hansebooks.com**

Frank D. Jackson

"Battle Flag Day"

August 10, 1894.

Ceremonials Attending the :
Transfer of the...

Battle Flags of Iowa Regiments

From the Arsenal to the Capitol.

...Report...

Of the

Battle Flag Committee

Appointed by the

Twenty-fourth General Assembly

To Provide Cases and Transfer the

Iowa Battle Flags

From the Arsenal to the State Capitol.

Des Moines:
F. R. Conaway, State Printer.
1896.

State of Iowa,
Adjutant=General's Office.

DES MOINES, January 14, 1896.

To the Honorable General Assembly of Iowa:

GENTLEMEN—We have the honor to herewith submit, as the committee named therein, a report of our proceedings in carrying out the provisions of the following act of the Twenty-fourth General Assembly of Iowa, to-wit:

"Be it enacted by the General Assembly of the State of Iowa:

"SECTION 1. That the adjutant-general and the curator of historical collections, with the advice and consent of the executive council, shall cause the colors, standards and battle flags borne by Iowa regiments and batteries during the war of the rebellion to be placed in hermetically sealed glass cases, in such manner as to display them to the best advantage, and to preserve them as far as possible from all injury thereto, and place them in appropriate locations in the corridors of the capitol; so much of said corridors as may be necessary is hereby appropriated for the purpose.

"SEC. 2. The sum of three thousand dollars, or so much thereof as may be necessary, is hereby appropriated out of any fund in the state treasury not otherwise appropriated, for said purpose, and that all accounts for the same shall be audited by the executive council."

Approved April 7, 1892.

For the "Introduction" to this report, the acknowledgments of your committee are due to Maj. S. H. M. Byers.   Very respectfully,

Jno. R. Prime

Adjutant-General.

Charles Aldrich

Curator of Historical Collections.

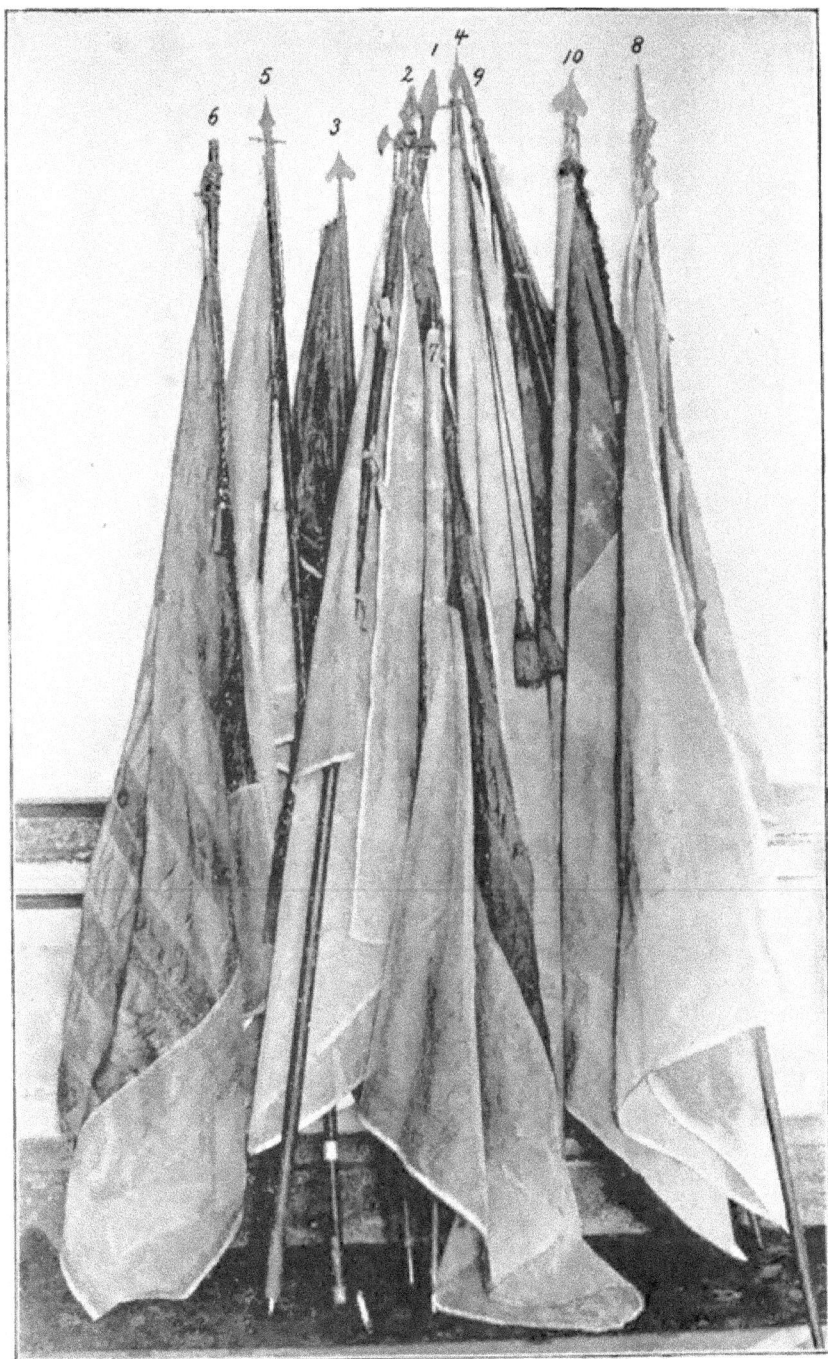

...Group One...

No. 1—First Cavalry.
No. 2—Second Infantry.
No. 3—Second Cavalry.
No. 4—First Battery.
No. 5—First Infantry.
No. 6—Third Infantry.
No. 7—Fourth Infantry.
No. 8—Fifth Infantry.
No. 9—Sixth Infantry.
No. 10—Seventh Infantry.

INTRODUCTION.

IT WAS a noble resolution that led to the proper preservation of Iowa's war flags. There was no danger of people forgetting the soldiers, or their sacrifices, but these flags, that were emblems of great deeds, might fade away. History hardly relates of another such scene as was witnessed in Iowa's capital on the 10th of August, 1894. That day saw the same soldiers who had carried the flags in battle bear them to their last resting place. It was thirty years nearly since the war—almost an average lifetime—and all these years the battle flags of the state had been hidden away in the old arsenal by the river. A few had been in museums; a few, honored as souvenirs of the great war, were treasured as so much gold in private homes, where happy children pointed to their shiny folds and said, "My father carried yonder flag." Now all the flags, banners, and guidons that had been through the war from Iowa were to be gathered together, and with acclaims of honor, and amidst tears and prayers, be borne to the capitol. It was a day to be remembered for a lifetime. So long as those who witnessed the touching spectacle live, they will recall to their own hearts, and tell to their children, how they saw 5,000 veteran soldiers of the great war come and march again under the flags they once bore in battle. They will tell you of the pathos of the scene—of the white-haired men, who, in their youth, had borne these flags in the fierce storm of conflict. now again taking them in their hands and blessing them and kissing them. The heart throbs and suppressed tears of many a soldier touching again the folds of these flags never will be known. There were mothers looking on whose sons lay dead on southern battle fields: and sisters whose brothers filled nameless graves in dark forests of the south. "My boy fell defending that flag," said an old man standing at the street-side. as the banner of his son's regiment passed by. The crowd about him gave way till the color-bearer could let the old man touch the sacred colors with his hands. Many hearts beat quick and many eyes were wet with tears. Yet this was the scene repeated and repeated all along Locust street, from Fifth street to the bridge, and from the bridge to the capitol. Many a white-haired mother from country farm or village looked on in silence as some flag was borne by, and with swelling hearts, and tearful eyes, thought of him whose grave she had never seen.

Des Moines was filled with people, and the vast crowds that lined the streets where the flags were borne, had but a single thought. Patriotism and gratitude, and love of country swelled in every breast. There were no partisans. All men and women alike gazed on the tattered flags and thought of the past. They looked into the faces of the men marching and said. "These are they who stormed forts, charged batteries, waded through swamps, starved in southern prisons: their very blood this moment on the bullet ridden flags." None cheered, their hearts stirred too deep—they only felt—and a greater emotion few will ever feel this side of the grave. Here and there the little remnant of some army band played the very music to which these men kept step at Shiloh and Mission Ridge. The same drums. the same drummers, the same fifers, the tones that had been silent thirty years again caused the blood of the marching men to tingle as they touched elbows and with quickened step recalled the days when, as comrades and brothers, they went battleward to that same old tune.

Locust street for a solid mile was full of men thinking of other days. Where were the thousands who had touched elbows in the marching line, to that same music, to those same drums, thirty years ago?

Twenty-five thousand of Iowa's soldiers are dead. Every man marching on Locust street that day thought of a comrade who once marched at his side to that tune, but who now slept in his soldier grave. Ahead of them in the line they saw the flags, torn and tattered, that they had borne over some rampart blazing with cannon. Then the flag was new, shiny and glorious. Then they were making history, now they were memories—slowly receding to the past. The world does not wait; time does not wait; the soldiers had their day, their glory and their death. The spectators must have theirs, too. These thousands of youths lining the sidewalks are thinking of the deeds and the glory of these veterans, and they pant for deeds and glory of their own. Will they be as brave, as true, as noble, as patriotic as these who are bearing their flags for the last time forever? All the vast crowd are thinking of these things, and to many the spectacle before them is of spectres with their flags marching on to the end. In a sense they are bidding them good-bye forever. It is the final obsequies of men who have made history. They will lay their flags down at the capitol, and generations will look at them and say: "There are the signs of their glory, but they are gone."

The tinge of melancholy that seized on the multitudes of people almost silenced demonstration. Spite of the occasional cheers of soldiers on being handed the flags, spite of the drums and the bands in the procession, there was comparative silence, and a minor strain ran through every chord, touched every heart. The occasion was too great for noise; too many hearts throbbed with sad recollections, too many eyes filled with tears.

At the head of the procession rode the gray-haired Colonel Shaw, a soldier of two wars, a hero of his command, who rode with the blaze of musketry as coolly as now he rode to the capitol.

One hundred and thirty-five veterans walked in line bearing the old flags. Five thousand other gray-haired veterans, who had once defended these colors at the mouth of the deadly cannon, followed as a guard of honor, and what a guard it was!

The blood of these men still stained the honored folds of the flags. These banners had never known defeat. They had been borne in a hundred battles—across the works of many a fort, but dishonor had never touched one of them. It is a proud, a noble record for Iowa, that her flags were always flags of honor and of victory. They were, like Iowa soldiers, at the front everywhere.

When future generations shall gaze in silence upon the dim colors of the flags there in the capitol, let them reflect that eighty thousand Iowa men carried these emblems of a nation into battle, and that thirteen thousand heroes were maimed, slaughtered, or died in their defense. Let them reflect that no Iowa flag ever surrendered to equal numbers; that not one of these banners ever was held aloft in a war of subjugation, nor for state aggrandizement. They were the signs of our own preservation only—the symbols of a free people. They are dimmed, but by the blood of their defenders; and torn, but by a foe that thought more of human bondage than of the nation's life.

It was noticeable that no captured flags of the enemy were borne in the procession, yet Iowa men had captured more flags than she had regiments. Hatred of foemen, revenge, were forgotten. On the other hand, there was no silly and hypocritical longing for the love and good will of those who had shot down comrades, starved helpless prisoners, and well-nigh murdered a nation. "Let God judge them and let us forget them" was a sentiment of fathers and mothers whose sons sleep in the woods of Tennessee or in the sands of Andersonville. That these sons should be forgotten and their brave deaths condoned at such a moment, was a crime against human nature.

When Governor Jackson issued his proclamation declaring August the 10th a state holiday, that on that day the flags should be borne to the capitol in solemn, but glorious procession, there was universal gratitude and approval. It was the anniversary of the battle of Wilson's Creek, where Iowa's first blood was shed. It was decided that the battle flags at the arsenal should be taken possession of by the representatives of the Sons of Veterans and by them be handed over to the color-sergeants who had borne them in battle; they in their turn carried them with glad hearts to the lines of veteran soldiers waiting in line to receive them with tears and blessings. Many had not seen these flags since the bloody battle's charge when, lying on the field wounded, they gave faint cheers for the symbols of their glory.

Colonel Dungan, the lieutenant-governor of the state, had been selected to address the color-bearers at the arsenal, and his words teemed with patriotism and honor, for he too had been a noble soldier.

When it had been announced in the press that the old color-guards, the very men who bore these flags through the dreadful war, should be the very men to carry them now in their last procession, a glad cheer went up over the state. These brave men, hidden away, pursuing their simple avocations on farm or in country village, silent as to their heroic deeds in their youth, were almost forgotten by the busy age. Now they came forward and plead for their rights—the honored privilege of once more carrying the old flag and touching its fading folds with their hands and their lips. Many and many a letter reached the committee of arrangements pathetic and tender to tears, written without the elegancies of rhetoric or penmanship, yet tenderly, touchingly pleading that the writers might carry the flag once more before they died. And it was their right. Their inelegancies of rhetoric and spelling were good enough in the days when cannon were firing and muskets blazing, and men were wanted to carry these flags into hostile lines and over the walls of death. They were good enough now.

2

Thirty years had made a difference, too. They were young then; now many are old, some poor. The fleeting years had not allowed them to catch up with the opportunities they lost while absent serving their country.

Civilians went ahead and got rich—rich even on the misfortunes of war. These soldiers lost their chance—many their health—many even their savings of boyhood. To many in that line a grateful nation had given a pension—it helped keep the wolf from the door—and yet was not a drop in the bucket to the hardships, the losses, the calamities that followed serving in a four years' war.

In all this vast crowd there was none who did not rejoice in the help the nation had given, and who did not wish it had been more. There was no cry of fraud and big pensions; no people's servants in high places sneering at the cripples who had saved the country; no political sycophants and demagogues striving to reduce the soldiers' little income. Ah! had some snarling creature on that 10th of August raised his voice against pensioning the men who bore those flags he would have been stoned to death.

The day was hot and sultry, but spite of the heat the long line of veterans gladly took up its march escorted by the National Guard, by Sons of Veterans, by soldiers from other states, by civic organizations, by bands of music and by the governor of the commonwealth and all his military family. As the line crossed the river and approached the capitol, its war flags waving, its blue-coated and white-haired legions keeping step to the music they had heard in battle, it was a spectacle never to be forgotten. Once it was like the funeral of some great conqueror. Rome had scarcely seen so grand a spectacle, for her triumphal entries were the return of professional soldiers who waged war for conquest, and in whose train men were led to bondage. This line, solemnly, gloriously, marching to Iowa's capitol, was the fragments of an army that had fought for the perpetuity of free institutions. The slaves that marched in its line were slaves no longer, but free men who in the ranks of the union army had battled for country.

The splendid arches under which the column moved, though bearing the names of honorable battles, still spoke of peace—good will to men. Many of the private citizens of the city decorated their places of business in a way that told of their appreciation of the day and the patriotism of their hearts. Flags floated everywhere, yet no flags were looked at save those faded and torn in the procession of the soldiers.

When the marching line and the banners reached the east side of the capitol a great crowd of people already awaited them. The old flags and the color bearers and as many veterans as possible clustered together on the great east steps, where they were photographed, that children's children may know something of how their fathers and the flags looked on this day, greatest of all in Iowa's history. Then commenced the speaking exercises of the occasion.

The committee on general arrangements had consisted of Gen. John R. Prime, the adjutant-general of the state; Capt. Charles Aldrich, curator of the historical society; Philip Schaller, department commander; Capt. C. H. Smith and Capt. J. P. Patrick, and by invitation, George A. Newman, commander of the Iowa Grand Army of the Republic. The secretary was Charles L. Longley, of the department of the Grand Army of the Republic.

At different committee meetings everything had been arranged that could tend to make the day one of great honor, and now followed the opening address by the president of the day, Gen. J. W. Noble, himself one of Iowa's distinguished soldiers.

Des Moines Union band followed with its strains of loyal music. There was a fervent invocation by the Rev. A. V. Kendrick, National Chaplain of the G. A. R., and an original poem by S. H. M. Byers, entitled "The Battle Flags of Iowa," and then came the principal address of the day, on the "Returning of the Flags," by Maj. John F. Lacey, member of congress, and a gallant officer of the old army. The response was by his excellency, Frank D. Jackson, governor of the state. Both

addresses were listened to with joy and were received by
the attending thousands with demonstrations of satisfaction.

Martial music by Carper's drum corps followed the
speeches, and Mrs. Jesse Cheek, of Des Moines, closed
the exercises by singing the "Star Spangled Banner."

Now the flags were in the golden-domed capitol, in
glass cases, hermetically sealed. There they will remain
forever, where patriots can look upon them in ages to
come. It was a fit place, in this noble building, this just
pride of a great state, to put these honored and priceless
treasures. In rooms near them are the written records
of these soldiers' deeds; their enlistment papers; their
discharges—Ah, too oft the records of their deaths. No
patriot looking upon them but his heart will throb faster
and truer; and no recollection of the war but will call up
the memory of those two great patriots and public servants, Adjutant-General Baker and Governor Kirkwood,
who put these records here and who did more than all
other public men of Iowa to make the path of an Iowa
soldier a path of honor. Near by, too, stands that noble
monument erected by a grateful people in honor of what
these men did to save their country. What trio of war
could more appropriately be together—these blood-
stained flags, these glorious records, this monument of
bronze and stone? And when gazing on them, let no
future patriot forget the words of that great war governor when he said: "The heroism of our soldiers has
made it a proud privilege to be a citizen of Iowa."

That many of these war flags had been preserved to
be honored on this great occasion had been due to the
patriotic thoughtfulness of an Iowa woman. When Sen-
ator John H. Gear was governor of Iowa, his wife saw
these flags being destroyed by dust and time. With her
own hands and with the aid of a few friends she tenderly
covered each one with a fabric that should protect them
and hold them together. The act was typical of the
universal patriotism of Iowa women in war times. The
women of Iowa made many of these flags, and with

tears and blessings gave them to husbands, brothers, sons, and lovers to carry into the war for the preservation of the country.

It is the proud satisfaction of a whole people to know that these flags were never dishonored—that they were bravely, nobly borne through four years of terrible conflict, and at last returned to the state stained with the patriotic blood of heroes.

These flags belong to the women of the state not less than to the men. Their unrecorded sacrifices were not of blood, but of human hearts. Let them, too, share in the glory that these illustrious flags cast upon the state.

...Group Two...

No. 1—Third Cavalry.
No. 2.—Fourth Cavalry.
No. 3—Second Battery.
No. 4—Thirteenth Infantry.
No. 5—Tenth Infantry.
No. 6—Eleventh Infantry.
No. 7—Eighth Infantry.
No. 8—Twelfth Infantry.
No. 9—Ninth Infantry.
No. 10—Fourteenth Infantry.

Governor's Proclamation.

Official Program.

Address of Hon. Warren S. Dungan, Lieutenant-Governor, on Delivering the Flags to the Color-Bearers at the Arsenal.

August 10, 1894.

A PROCLAMATION.

HE Twenty-fourth General Assembly of the state of Iowa enacted a law providing for the better preservation of the colors, standards and battle flags borne by Iowa regiments and batteries during the war of the rebellion. In compliance with the provisions of said law, hermetically sealed glass cases have been provided and placed in appropriate positions in the corridor of the capitol, in which the battle flags will be preserved. The 10th day of August, 1894, has been selected as an appropriate day for the transfer of the battle flags from the state arsenal to the capitol building. This great occasion, one of the last official acts of our state in patriotic remembrance of that heroic army which she sent forth to defend the flag while yet in the very infancy of her statehood, is one in which every true citizen of Iowa will be deeply interested. The hardships and sacrifices, the alternating victories and defeats, and the final triumph and after glory of that army are matters of history; but the battle-flags around which our Iowa soldiers rallied, and under the folds of which they marched through smoke of battle to victory or death, are left to us, a precious heritage toward which the hearts of all Iowans go forth in grateful remembrance.

Now, therefore, I, Frank D. Jackson, governor of the state of Iowa, do hereby recommend that the 10th day of August, 1894, be known and referred to as Battle Flag Day, and that it be observed as a public holiday consecrated to the memory of the patriotism and valor of Iowa's soldiers, living and dead.

Let the subject of patriotism, as represented in the one hundred and thirty-three flags that led the seventy thousand Iowa soldiers into battle, be the inspiring sentiment of the day, and I hereby request that all the people of this commonwealth refrain upon that day from unnecessary labor and join in appropriate exercises in commemoration of this patriotic occasion.

Let as many as possible of the surviving members of Iowa regiments take a personal part in the exercises of this day. Let regimental reunions be called to meet at the capital city on the day previous, so that as far as possible these battle flags may be carried by their own respective color bearers, surrounded by the broken fragments of regimental organization.

With a spirit of reverent solemnity, let the people of Iowa devote this day to the consideration of the relations of the citizen to the flag; of liberty as distinct from license; of loyalty, patriotism and heroism. Let us again renew our devotion to the flag—our fidelity to the law.

IN TESTIMONY WHEREOF, I have hereunto set my hand and caused to be affixed the great seal of the state of Iowa.

Done at Des Moines this twenty-eighth day of June, in the year of our Lord, one thousand eight hundred and ninety-four.

Frank D Jackson

By the Governor:

OFFICIAL ANNOUNCEMENT FOR BATTLE FLAG DAY.

THE governor of Iowa having, by his proclamation, designated August 10, 1894, as battle flag
day, and the day on which the flags and banners carried by Iowa regiments and batteries
during the war of the rebellion, would be
transferred from the arsenal to the cases provided for their reception in the capitol building, the following announcement of the order
of exercises for the day is made by the committee on arrangements for the information of all interested.

The line will be formed for the parade promptly at 1 o'clock
P. M., in the following order:

PLATOON OF POLICE.
DES MOINES UNION BAND.
GOVERNOR AND STAFF.

FIRST DIVISION.

MAJOR JOHN C. LOPER, COMMANDING.
COMPANY "H," THIRD REGIMENT, I. N. G.
COMPANY "A," THIRD REGIMENT, I. N. G.
BOYS' BRIGADE.
SONS OF VETERANS.

SECOND DIVISION.

GEO. A. NEWMAN, DEPARTMENT COMMANDER, COMMANDING
DEPARTMENT OF IOWA, G. A R.,
INCLUDING ALL EX-SOLDIERS, SAILORS, AND MARINES, OTHER
THAN IOWA SOLDIERS, WHETHER MEMBERS OF THE
GRAND ARMY OF THE REPUBLIC OR NOT.
MAJOR CARPER'S DRUM CORPS.

THIRD DIVISION.

Colonel William T. Shaw, Commanding.

General H. H. Wright, Aid.

Captain C. H. Smith, Aid.

Iowa Soldiers, Sailors and Marines, with Battle Flags.

The column being formed will proceed to the arsenal, where the battle flags and banners will be delivered to the color-bearers of the respective regiments and batteries by Lieutenant-Governor Warren S. Dungan, late Lieutenant-Colonel of the Thirty-fourth Iowa Volunteer Infantry, and thence to the capitol building, where the following exercises will be held:

1. Call to Order, - Gen. J. W. Noble, Presiding Officer.
2. Music, - - - Des Moines Union Band.
3. Invocation, - - - Rev. A. V. Kendrick.
4. Original Poem, - - Major S. H. M. Byers.
5. Address, - "Returning Flags to the State."
Major John F. Lacey.
6. Response, - - Governor Frank D. Jackson.
7. Martial Music, - - Carper's Drum Corps.
8. Song, - - - "Star Spangled Banner."
Mrs. Jesse Cheek.

The railroads of Iowa have granted the usual rate of one fare for the round trip from all points in the state to Des Moines, tickets to be on sale August 8th, 9th and 10th, up to the time of the exercises, and good returning August 11th.

It is most desirable that all Iowa soldiers who can possibly do so, arrive in Des Moines as early as practicable Thursday, August 9th, for the purpose of perfecting regimental organizations, preparatory to the formation of the parade on the following day, by the selection of regimental commanders and color-bearers.

Upon arriving in Des Moines all Iowa soldiers should report as soon as possible at the adjutant-general's office in the capitol building, where rooms will be provided for the purpose of holding regimental meetings.

Crocker and Kinsman Posts, G. A. R., of Des Moines, having generously taken an active interest in the matter, the committee can assure all comrades who come that they will be able to obtain good accommodations at reasonable prices.

Comrades, come! It is the last opportunity we shall have to march under the folds of these sacred, battle-scarred emblems of the patriotism and valor of Iowa soldiers, living and dead.

Come join us once more in doing honor, in peace, to the dear old flags that were never dishonored in war.

JNO. R. PRIME,
CHARLES ALDRICH,
PHIL. SCHALLER,
C. H. SMITH,
J. P. PATRICK,
Committee.

LIEUT.-GOV. DUNGAN'S SPEECH

On Delivering the Flags to Old Color-Bearers at the Arsenal.

COMRADES, survivors of that splendid army of over 75,000 men, furnished by the state of Iowa during the great rebellion: This day is to the whole people of the state, and especially to you, a day of absorbing interest—a day to become historic in the annals of our beloved state. You have been called together by the proclamation of the governor of the state, for the purpose of removing these old battle flags, borne by you and your comrades on so many sanguinary battle fields, during that momentous struggle, from their present resting place in this arsenal to the place prepared for them in the corridors of the new capitol of the state, for their better preservation.

The sight of these dear old flags stirs your souls to their very depths. They awaken afresh in your memories the thrilling scenes of a third of a century ago. The whole panorama of that great war passes in review before you. You hear anew the startling sound of an enemy's artillery firing upon a United States fort. You feel again the depths of that emotion which stirred the hearts of all loyal citizens to realize the danger which threatened the union, and awakened in your hearts the patriotic resolve to swear anew allegiance to the old flag and to offer your services, and your lives, if need be, to preserve the union bequeathed to us by the fathers of the republic.

3

You recall the hour of the greatest trial experienced in your soldier life—the hour of parting from your wife and child; or from father and mother, sisters and brothers, or your sweetheart.

You remember the shout which greeted the first flag received by your regiment as it was unfurled to the breeze in your sight. It was perhaps the gift of the patriotic women of your own neighborhood. The Thirty-fourth Iowa regiment, to which I belonged, went into camp at Burlington. The patriotic women of that city presented us with our first regimental flag.

In doing so they charged us to bear it bravely in the face of the foe, and never allow it to be trailed in the dust or to be dishonored. We pledged them life, fortune and honor to obey their injunction This was an inspiration which the regiment could never forget. How well our pledges were redeemed history must record. An evidence of our fidelity, however, is seen in this battle-scarred flag—the one they presented to us, and one of the three flags the Thirty-fourth furnished to the collection before us. If I remember aright, the patriotic women of Burlington presented the First Iowa cavalry and perhaps other regiments with their first regimental flag.

Comrades, you recall the battles in which you were engaged and in which the stars and stripes were your inspiration to noble deeds. You bore them until they were torn and tattered, often bullet-riven and blood-stained, until no longer fit for service, and then, with careful hands, you folded them up and sent them to the adjutant-general of the state for safe keeping, where you find them to-day.

In recalling the heroic deeds witnessed by you in your army life, nothing swells your breasts with greater pride than to remember the devotion of the color-guard to the flags and standards in their keeping. Their heroism was witnessed on many a battle field. One color-bearer is shot down and another springs to his place, raises the fallen flag and moves forward only to fall as the first, until sometimes three or four have fallen in a single battle. Witness the Second Iowa at Fort Donelson: the fourth color-bearer falls, but is able to rise and bear the flag to the end of the fight and to victory. And that color-bearer is with us to-day in the person of Comrade Twombly, late treasurer of state. Many instances of a similar character might be enumerated, but time will not permit.

Comrades, your hearts may well beat with honest pride to-day when you remember how gallantly you bore these flags at Wilson's Creek, Vicksburg, Donelson, Lookout Mountain, Mission Ridge, Atlantic, Mobile, Blakely. Gettysburg. the Wilderness, Fredericksburg, and on to victory at Appomatox. You kept your pledges to the noble women who presented you so many of these flags. Our flags have never been lowered or disgraced by an Iowa regiment; a few of our flags were captured by the enemy, but the troops that bore them were facing the foe defending them with undaunted courage. Here are the great body of the flags we carried to battle and to victory, our witnesses to the people this day.

Look upon them! Not only battle-scarred, but purple-stained with the blood of your fallen comrades They were placed here for safe keeping, but soon they began to fade and waste away. Seeing this. the patriotic care of an Iowa woman partly with her own hands, encased them in tarlton for their preservation—the wife of the then governor—Mrs. John H. Gear. This was a partial protection, but it was evident that they could not long be kept intact unless otherwise cared for. Iowa is proud of the record made by her citizen soldiery. She has shown this by many liberal laws on her statute books. Proud of her military record and of the fidelity, valor and patriotism of her sons and regarding these flags as the best evidence of that record, of that valor and patriotism, and viewing their possession as a sacred trust, she has prepared receptacles in the rotunda of our new capitol for their deposit, consisting of hermetically sealed glass cases, where, it is hoped, they may be preserved in their present condition for long years if not for ages to come. There they will be in a position where the whole people of the state may look upon them as often as they pass through the capitol, patriotic object lessons, not only to the present generation. but to our children and to our children's children down the ages.

Color bearers, yours is the post of honor to-day; you take these old flags in your hands for the last time; you carry them to the capitol and deliver them into the hands of the governor of the state who, on behalf of the state, receives them at your hands and sees to their proper deposit.

Comrades with us in the great struggle for the union who served in regiments from other states, we are glad to welcome you with us on this occasion. To you is equal honor due for the triumph of our cause. Being now citizens of Iowa, we know that you share with us the just pride we feel in preserving, as long as possible, our revered old battle flags.

Citizens of Iowa, your presence with us signifies your deep interest in all that pertains to the honor and welfare of our beloved state. Your loyalty to both the state and nation has ever been conspicuous. Your devotion to the flag has never faltered, and your regard for the union soldier has been constant. We are proud of the fact that the whole people of the state unite with us in our care for these battle flags, and share with us the honors and the responsibilities of their safe preservation.

One very sad thought forces itself upon us as we gaze at these battle-scarred and blood-stained banners—the thought that so many of the gallant men who carried them to battle and to victory were not permitted to return with them. All honor to the noble dead who "died that the nation might live." And are they dead to us? An Iowa poet has said:

"There is no death! The stars go down
  To rise upon some fairer shore,
And bright in heaven's jeweled crown
  To shine forever more.

There is no death! The dust we tread
  Shall change beneath the summer showers
To golden rain or mellow fruit,
  Or rainbow-tinted flowers.

There is no death! An angel form
  Walks o'er the earth with silent tread—
He bears our best loved things away,
  And then we call them dead."

They shall live in our hearts and memories and in history, so long as patriotism continues to be the crowning virtue of good citizenship.

...Group Three...

No. 1—Fifth Cavalry.
No. 2—Seventh Cavalry.
No. 3—Third Battery.
No. 4—Fifteenth Infantry.
No. 5—Sixteenth Infantry.
No. 6—Seventeenth Infantry.
No. 7—Eighteenth Infantry.
No. 8—Nineteenth Infantry.
No. 9—Twentieth Infantry.
No. 10—Twenty-first Infantry.

Exercises and Addresses

At the Capitol.

EXERCISES AND ADDRESSES.

GENERAL JOHN W. NOBLE, formerly colonel of the Third Veteran Volunteer Cavalry regiment of Iowa, was introduced by Adjutant-General Prime, to be presiding officer of ceremonies at Des Moines, Iowa, battle flag day, August 10, 1894, and spoke as follows:

Comrades and Fellow Citizens: In calling this meeting to order, I wish first to acknowledge the great honor conferred upon me by your selection of myself as presiding officer. I must refer it rather to your partiality than to any claims of mine to distinction among so many eminent and war-worn veterans. It would have been honor enough for me to have met with you on this great battle flag day, to have recalled the days of our united service for our country, and know that I too was an Iowa soldier. I thank you and ask your kind assistance in discharging the duties of the hour.

By authority of the state, given by act and resolution of the legislature, and in pursuance of the proclamation of the governor, we have assembled to place the battle flags borne by the soldiers of Iowa in the war for the union, here in the capitol and the custody of the people forever.

It is a solemn, it may be said, sacred occasion, for around these flags what memories cling, and by their presence what thoughts and emotions are called forth. Military achievement and glory may swell the heart with the consciousness of victory, but the lapse of time cannot efface the sadness we must ever feel for the loss and sacrifice of those who held those banners aloft in the battle.

Said a sergeant, Lowe, of the Thirtieth regiment, when shot
through the body at Kenesaw: "Tell my father and brothers
that whenever they see the stars and stripes to remember that
I died for the brave old flag."

In many different regiments assaulting the foe on varied
fields of the war. man after man, when one was shot another
springing forward, bore these flags onward, with the all but
absolute knowledge that death would be the result. We know
the glorious lives of these standards: what lives they cost; what
lives and what liberty with the power of our union they saved.

But it is not for me to-day to cite the record or speak at
length of their history. Others will recount them appropriately. All that may be said will be, however, but the renewal
of memories to you, for they are your flags, and their history
is your history. You, yes, let me say my comrades, we are the
remnants of those who went forth with these banners, and our
hearts will be cold and our tongues forever silent ere we shall
cease to feel and celebrate the services, the suffering, the glory
and the success of the Iowa soldiers, and claim for them and
their equally deserving comrades of the other states who stood
shoulder to shoulder with them, the gratitude and recognition
of our united people.

A third of a century ago the regiments of Iowa went forth
to battle for the constitution and the union. The enterprise
and intelligence of the eastern, and middle, and other states
had peopled Iowa's cities and prairies. Than her soldiers,
none were more loyal and daring. Her volunteers represented
fully the worth of Iowa's property, education and patriotism.
Her arms were supported by a well matured and vigorous man-
hood, and her courage by a nervous force and mental training
unsurpassed among all the hosts that marched to the front.
They were encouraged and supported. too, by as God-fearing
and land-loving a people at home, a people as elevated in sentiment and pure in life, as this world has known; free as the
northwest wind that fanned them, and strong as the currents
of the great rivers that bounded their territory and nourished
their land, forcing their ways through a continent to the sea.
There was no reason these volunteers should fail in duty, and
there was every incentive to the marked and eminent success
they attained; alas! the achievement of death and suffering in
all forms known to war, but, proudly we say it, the attain-
ment of victory and the maintenance of the supremacy and

continuance of these United States. That service was grandly performed.

The First regiment of Iowa Volunteers, on August 10th, thirty-three years ago this day, sustained the brunt of the battle at Wilson's Creek, and thirteen other regiments, after braving and achieving all that to have served with Grant and Sherman implies, went on the march to the sea, and were at the close of the war in the grand review at Washington. Sheridan knew other of our regiments as among his most reliable in the great campaign of the Shenandoah valley, as he had long before gained his first distinction in connection with an Iowa cavalry regiment in Tennessee. Who that speaks of Donelson, Pittsburg Landing, Iuka or Corinth, Raymond, Champion Hill, Black River or Vicksburg, Lookout Mountain, Missionary Ridge, Resaca, Allatoona, Kenesaw and Atlanta, Savannah or Columbia, Winchester, Cedar Creek or Fisher's Hill, Red River or Mobile, Montevallo, Ebenezer Church, Selma and Columbus, Franklin, Nashville, Blue Mills, Wilson's Creek, Kirksville, Springfield, Pea Ridge or Prairie Grove, Osage and Independence, or any of the fields of the west and south: who that marks the rise to greatness and renown of the most distinguished of our generals: who that knows how the shackles, placed upon the commerce of the Mississippi, were burst asunder, and its avenues once more opened from river shore to ocean coast: who that reckons up the courage and endurance and all-pervading love of country that met at every point the advancing and boasting hosts of secession and disloyalty: who that estimates the most important factors that maintained the constitution and sustained the flag, but must and gladly does recognize the continued and most efficient services, from the first to the last of the war for the union, of gallant, devoted and heroic sons of Iowa?

We are now to place in shrines of safety the battle flags of these troops. How bright they were when they went forth: with what loving and patient hearts the mothers and daughters, sweethearts and wives gave them to the keeping of men then young and full of hope, but all alike volunteering life and fortune for God and humanity. How soon the bloody record of that sacrifice began; how constantly it increased. The roll of battle and death came sullenly on through the long four years. But our flags were still there. And though every shell or bomb that rent the regiment on the field went on until it desolated a hearthstone away back in this fair state, the ranks were firmly closed again, and the sobs of affection were smothered in prayers for the flag. How the havoc increased; how dreadful was the number of the dead; how, even now, the soul shrinks at the recital of their names. But it was for the land we love; it was to do or die for our country. The re-enlistments came; experience had shown the reality and sternness of the duty originally assumed in the first outburst of enthusiasm, but the cause had not yet been won. It was a war of principle. The flags were still there, the symbols of that principle, and they were to remain there until wreathed with victory. The support from home was redoubled; the gray beards went to guard duty at points distant from home, and from the state. The sanitary commission and hospital nurses strove to render the camp more endurable, and soothe and support the sick and wounded. The colored troops were organized and officered by Iowa soldiers. But the thought to give over the strife came never to any in Iowa.

There was to be but one result—the supremacy of the national government. The union as it was and shall ever be.

Victory came at last in every state and on every field. The regiments returned. Their dead, how many! and sleeping how far away! But ever to be remembered as those who had given the highest proof of constancy. The wounded and the wasted returned, and were enfolded to the heart of a grateful state and nation, and never will it be possible to reward them too highly. One of the brightest pages of American history will be that of the gratitude of our people for its veterans

And the flags were borne home again and inscribed with names of successful battles for the republic that have passed into history as the most skillful military achievements for the worthiest cause the world has ever known.

And here are the flags!

Over them is the capitol of Iowa, and over all the constitution of the United States.

The work of the fathers has been preserved. The generation that supported it is passing away as the generation that created it has long since departed.

Men may die, but principles never. The love of representative republican government, of constitutional freedom, is as strong to-day among our people as it ever was. The government that put down the great rebellion against the constitution is as strong as ever, and its people love it as they ever have. It will not be surrendered to insurrection; to unauthorized assumption of authority, or to the supercilious presumption of individuals.

The great guarantees of life, liberty and prosperity, wrought out by so much sacrifice, will be preserved and enforced under the constitution as it is, and the instrumentalities it controls. It is capable and its energy will meet and surpass every peril.

> "Fear not each sudden sound and shock,
> It is of the wave and not the rock."

It will prevail—"the least as feeling its care, and the greatest as not exempt from its power."

These flags will tell to the rising generations of Iowa, what their fathers and mothers did and suffered. Other like symbols will be borne into many a civil, and it may be, military contest by our immediate successors and their posterity. Rent and stained they too will be placed away in honor as we to-day enshrine those here, but there will be ever floating from the summit of the capitol that one supreme symbol of our national glory which, though fresh and new, and dancing on the soft winds of summer, will be prouder because it has met adversity; brighter because it has been blackened by battle and blood; and there ever cheerfully waving in those future years and ages, because it is "the flag of the free hearts' only home" and the emblem of constitutional American liberty.

Comrades, I call this meeting to order.

Attention! Battalions!

Following General Noble's address the Des Moines Union band rendered some appropriate music, after which Rev. A. V. Kendrick delivered an eloquent and impressive invocation, following which Major S. H. M. Byers read the following original poem:

THE BATTLE FLAGS OF IOWA.

BY S. H. M. BYERS.

Tread softly here. 'Tis valor's home:
    Sons of a noble west;
Beneath the splendors of this dome
    'Tis fit your banners rest.
Oh! remnant of a mighty host
    That marshalled for the fray,
Nor feared war's dreadful holocaust,
    Be welcome here to-day.

Bear once again the flags ye bore
    'Midst howling shot and shell,
And squadrons' charge and cannons' roar,
    And shrieks and shouts of hell;
And touch you silken flags again,
    And kiss yon shining stars,
And hold them to your breast as when
    You held them in the wars.

Rewaken memories of the past
    That long have slumbered still,
And hear once more the bugle's blast,
    And feel the battle's thrill.
And hear again the shout, "they fly,"
    The cry the victors gave—
Oh! never yet was such a cry
    Heard this side of the grave.

And if some comrade's heart blood stain
    The tattered stripes and stars,
And naught of the old flag remain
    But faded battle scars—
Think not 'twas vain that comrade stood,
    His sacrifice too high—
For every drop of freedom's blood
    Is written in the sky.

The angels meet with smiling eyes
    The comrades that ye gave,
And welcome into Paradise
    The spirits of the brave ;
And whether in the battle's smoke,
    Or in some prison drear,
God's angels heard the hearts that broke,
    And answered with a tear.

Oh! stars and stripes of Donelson,
And Shiloh's bloody flags,
Think ye there's naught of all ye won
Save these poor faded rags?
Th'nk ye no memories of the past
Can stir our hearts to-day?
Nor cry "to arms," nor bugle's blast,
Nor battle's fierce array?

Oh! banners that Atlanta knew
And Vicksburg's frowning heights.
With bloody hands they welcomed you
In half a hundred fights.
Think ye the hands that bore you then
On Chattanooga's brow.
On Corinth's field, and Belmont's plain.
Can be forgotten now?

Cursed, doubly cursed, who would forget
That these torn banners here
With his own father's blood were wet.
With his own mother's tear:
That when on Lookout's heights was borne
Amidst the battle's shout
Yon stars and stripes, now old and torn,
His brother's life went out.

Oh! flags that never knew defeat.
Nor led a conquest war.
That waved o'er many a fort and fleet,
And never lost a star:
Come there not sometimes in the night,
When all the world is still,
The heroes of Iuka's fights.
The men of Champion's Hill?

Assemble round you once again.
In uniforms of blue,
A thousand spirits of the slain
That gave their lives for you?
From out their graves at Winchester
See ye their columns wheel?
From Pea Ridge, and from Wilson's Creek,
The stormers of Mobile?

Come they not smiling once again,
About your table-round,
To sit there in the moonlight, when
There is no battle sound?
All tell of dangers half forgot,
Of battles long since by,
And how for liberty tis 'not
So hard a thing to die?

Oh! land with patriots such as these
    Securely can'st thou rest—
And fear no foes, on land or seas,
    No traitors, east or west.
Oh! Thou that kept these heroes brave
    When the dark conflict came,
Make us but worthy what they gave,
    And worthy of their fame.

...Group Four...

No. 1—Twenty-second Infantry.
No. 2—Twenty-third Infantry.
No. 3—Twenty-fourth Infantry.
No. 4—Twenty-fifth Infantry.
No. 5—Twenty-sixth Infantry.
No. 6—Twenty-seventh Infantry.
No. 7—Twenty-eighth Infantry.
No. 8—Twenty-ninth Infantry.
No. 9—Thirtieth Infantry.
No. 10—Eighth Cavalry.

HON. JOHN F. LACEY'S ADDRESS

Returning the Flags to the Permanent Custody of the State.

ALTHOUGH nearly a third of a century has passed since the civil war, its battle flags are still the objects of popular love and devotion. And so we find a common patriotic impulse spontaneously moving towards their preservation. The legislature of Iowa has enacted this sentiment into law. Animated by the same spirit, private citizens and survivors of regiments having such flags in their custody have cheerfully added them to those heretofore held by the adjutant-general of the state.

The citizens of Iowa are now assembled to formally transfer to the keeping of the commonwealth as among its most sacred possessions the flags that Iowa courage and Iowa patriotism followed in defense of the union. To the safe keeping of our great commonwealth we entrust these banners. Their cost is priceless, and their history glorious beyond expression. As a soldier in the past and as a citizen and civilian in the present, to me has been accorded the honor of speaking for these mute trophies. Upon a soil dedicated to liberty forever, we meet to recall the memories with which these emblems shall be associated in history. Memories arise, tender, sad, fierce, exulting; but leading up in the end to forgiveness, reconciliation, unity and peace. These dumb memorials of the past are more eloquent than any spoken words. In their holy presence partisanship is silent and only sentiments of patriotism, wide as the nation itself, may rise to the lips. The nation is no longer welded by bands of iron and shafts of steel. The silken threads of these flags soothe and bind us together heart and soul as they rustle gently as the wings of doves in the free wind of heaven.

The motto of Iowa, inscribed by one of Iowa's honest sons upon
the great monument of Washington, never spoke the sentiments of her people more fully than they do to-day: "Iowa:
Her affections, like the rivers of her borders, flow to an insep-
arable union."

As we meet here to-day, to Almighty God our hearts should
be lifted in quiet but earnest gratitude. Let us have no malice
and indulge in no mere exultation over the victories which
render this celebration possible   To the erring states that
sought to rend that flag, to the brethren who sought to substi-
tute two rival and hostile nations for the friendly union of the
states, we give the old flag as their emblem as well as ours.
Many a star has been shot from the colors before us, but the
states which those stars represent never in fact have lost their
true and rightful places in the union.   It still remains an indis-
soluble union of indestructible states. With high and patriotic
spirit let us trace the history of our star-spangled banner.
Flags are chosen to speak for those who carry them. We
shoot at a hostile standard and salute a friendly one. The stars
and stripes were chosen as the national ensign, September 3,
1777, and in eight days afterwards floated over the victorious
field of Brandywine and soon after graced the surrender of
Burgoyne. They cheered Washington at Valley Forge and
waved proudly over Yorktown when independence triumphed
at the last. This flag of thirteen stripes and a union with blue
with as many white stars as there are states in the union, took
its present precise form April 4, 1818. But new as it is, it is
already ancient among the banners of the world. It is older
than the present flags of France, Spain, England and Germany.
But if we measure its age by the deeds that it glorifies, it would
run back into an antiquity remote indeed. It was carried to
the utmost southern point by American enterprise when the
Antarctic continent at the south pole was discovered. It has
been planted at the highest latitude on the edge of the open
sea that looks forever in solemn silence at the motionless polar
star. It has been borne by a Stanley to the sources of the
Congo and the Nile, where it greeted the enduring, daring and
patient Livingston in the chosen scenes of his self-sacrificing
attempt to Christianize the very depths of degradation and
human slavery. Over the sea, in every port, it has gladdened
the sky. It has been planted alike on earth's wildest and most

inaccessible peak, and upon the sea's remotest and most solitary shore.

A stranger may look upon these emblems and say: "What are they anyhow? Nothing but flags—nothing but a few pieces of silk—some red and white stripes—some white stars in a blue field—and that is all."

"A primrose by the river's brim.
A yellow primrose is to him:
And it is nothing more."

We do not analyze a tear, but think rather of the emotions of joy or grief that bid it flow. The stripes, the stars, the silk or the bunting, are the material things a flag is made of but the love, the hopes, the memories of the people, which are symbolized by their national banner, are the true flag after all. They constitute its soul A woven or embroidered eagle, a cross, a crown, a dragon, a lion: or some imaginary beast or bird taken from the field of heraldry became the badges of the nations of the olden time. But the new and bright republic in its day of early hope and faith, appealed to heaven, and looking up into the sky choose the stars themselves as the emblem of the land of the free and the home of the brave.

In the capitals of Europe the stranger looks upon the crown jewels as typical of the pride and glory of ancient monarchies. But here the pilgrim finds no material thing so prized as the country's flag, and none so dear as the battle flag of the republic. The splendid capitol of two millions of people will hold no treasure more worthy of its keeping than the banners we deposit here to-day.

At one time they gleamed in the sunlight fresh and beautiful, their colors as bright as the flowers of the prairies, and he who looked upon their array could realize how "terrible was an army with banners." But to-day they are dearer than when bright and gorgeous they were intrusted to the keeping of the young soldiers of our state. They have been carried without dishonor, they are returned without disgrace: on their silken folds are inscribed the names of many battles in which they have been borne in defense of national existence, and the record is one in which all who participated may take an honest pride Those names are crumbling with decay. but the results of these battles are projected into the history of the world, and countless ages will yet feel their influence. The victory was not the triumph of Iowa, nor of the North, but of the whole union, and in the future of our united country the stars of the south will shine with the same lustre as those of the north.

From the center to the sea the true American looks only for what is best for all of our common and reunited family.

The riotous anarchist may raise his voice and defy the power of the government for a day, but the mighty nation, serene in its strength, confident in its honor, erect in its justice, calls for peace and obedience and its order is obeyed.

To the youth here let me say: Do you know what these flags mean? They mean a nation saved, its unity upheld, its honor preserved, its power unbroken, and all men in its borders forever free. Do you know, my young friend, how many men have died defending these colors? Around these banners as centers have raged the tempests of fire in the greatest battles. From 1861 to 1865 Iowa was not the mighty commonwealth of 2,000,-000 souls that she is to-day. Her railways and her cities were only in embryo. But from her sparsely settled prairies 76,242 men enlisted in the army of the union. Nine regiments of cavalry and four batteries of artillery bore these guidons. Forty-eight regiments of white and one of black infantry carried the name and fame of Iowa in the great campaigns and battles of the rebellion. Before the war ended 12 368 men, the youngest, the strongest and bravest, lay in their graves, and 8,848 were shot in the defense of these very flags which you honor to-day. Disease has made fierce havoc in those ranks in the days of peace, and now age is striking its certain blows upon the grey-headed column that still remains. Thousands of miles of weary, dusty and dangerous march are here recorded. Through the pestilence of the swamp, by the deadly ambush, in every compaign the standard of the Iowa soldier was borne where duty called. In the clouds of Lookout Mountain and the fogs of Yazoo, by the Shenandoah and the Mississippi; under Sheridan or Grant; under Hooker or Dodge; under Rice or Crocker; under Sherman or Canby; under Wilson or Noble; under A. J. Smith or Steele; under the gallant leaders that I cannot take the time to name, wherever danger lurked and men of courage were needed, Iowa men were given the post of honor. Some Iowa flags were captured, but their loss was never coupled with dishonor. Their capture cost the captors dear. So glorious was our defense that our enemies, now our brethren, have sent them back to be carried in this memorial of peace.

And here they are to-day on this anniversary of the battle of
Wilson's Creek, and a day that brings a flush of honest pride
to the cheek of every citizen of the Hawkeye state, and recalls
a gallant regiment voluntarily remaining beyond its term of
enlistment to stand by Lyon on that bloody field to teach the
world what Iowa troops were made of. We look with full heart
and swimming eyes upon these colors in their last march.

Rains have drenched them;
Powder smoke has stained them;
Storms have tried and torn them;
The tooth of time has eaten them;
Age has faded them.

But the glory of the deeds they commemorate will never
fade from earth. They are but fragments of silk, frayed, soiled
and torn in a hundred battles and marches, but they represent
those scenes by flood and field where the struggle for peace and
union were fought, and fought to the end. The very stars in
their courses fought for union and liberty. When soldiers defy
death they drive him into the ranks of the enemy, and men defy
death when they fight under the banner of their choice for the
land they love. To the dead who fell by land and sea we give
honor to-day. This festival of the flags is one of special honor
to the dead, and to none more so than those gallant men whose
last resting place is unknown. In a single tomb at Arlington
are deposited the remains of over 2,000 of these unknown
heroes.

When Iowa's beautiful monument, in honor of her soldiers,
arises near this capitol, let there be inscribed a tablet to her
unknown dead. With the soldiers of foreign birth who laid
down or hazarded their lives for the land of their adoption,
and with the black man who dared death for the government
which had done him nothing but wrong, we share to-day the
honors of victory and the benefits of a free and united country.

A nation's emblem should be appropriate. Ours is the stars
of heaven. The confederacy chose the southern cross to adorn
its battle flag, a constellation invisible even from the most
southern limits of the United States. Australia, with inverted
seasons and alien sky, might well adopt this group of stars as
its standard, but it was not a fitting symbol for any part of the
American union. To the men who fought against us then we
now extend the hand of fellowship. For their gallant dead we
sorrow as well as for our own.

"Under the sod and the dew,
  Waiting the judgment day,
Under the laurel the blue,
  Under the willow the gray."

Theirs was a misplaced sentiment which put the state against the nation. Our soldiers loved Iowa no less, but they loved the nation more, and we rejoice that we are brothers once again. Out of all this turmoil and strife good has come in the providence of God. From the body of the lion honey was taken, and from the tunnel at Andersonville dug by our soldiers in an unavailing attempt at freedom, flows now a perpetual spring amid the graves of a national cemetery. And in the recent domestic troubles through which we have just passed, the quiet loyalty of the states so lately arrayed against the government has been a gratifying and pleasing spectacle.

But while we forgive and accept the erring states back again into the power as well as the benefits of peace and unity, we will never fail to teach that the cause of the union and liberty was then and will be forever right. Let us forgive but remember.

To the prisoner of war nothing was so dear as the flag of his country, and on returning from the hostile lines its sight has cheered many a soldier's heart, and made him forget his hunger and his rags. Let me recall an incident. On the fourth day of July, 1863, when Pemberton was marching out with the disarmed defenders of Vicksburg, when Meade was following up his victory at Gettysburg and the hills of Helena were echoing with the repulse of Price and Holmes, the prisoners at Libby wanted to celebrate the day of independence. Surrounded by guards on all sides, to celebrate the Fourth of July had its difficulties, and among them was the fact that no flag floated in Richmond but the hated confederate standard. To celebrate independence day without the stars and stripes seemed like a hollow mockery. The old flag must be had at all hazards, and three soldiers, one wearing a red shirt, another a white, and a third a blue one, stripped themselves in the cause of patriotism and the day was celebrated with no feature omitted. The captive ensign fluttering within the prison walls spoke of home, of country and liberty. The materials were humble, but the flag was worthy of taking its place among the sacred memorials we are about to deposit here to-day.

By the presence of these colors I am reminded of the tender memory of Nathaniel B. Baker, adjutant-general of Iowa, and of the story he used to tell. To him is mainly due the gathering and preservation of these sacred relics. One day, in the early years after the war, as he was sitting in his office, which was decorated by these battle flags, a lady dressed in deep mourning came in and asked to see the flag of the Twentieth Iowa. The general pointed it out to her and she stood for awhile in silence and meditation. It hung above her reach. "May I touch it?" she said, and General Baker moved a table below it, upon which she climbed, and, pressing the silken folds to her bosom and lips, she burst into tears and said: "Pardon my emotion, General, but my only boy died under this flag."

Here, I am told (for I have not counted them), we have 138 flags of all kinds. They are about to be delivered to the governor of Iowa and his successors in office, as a sacred trust. Henceforth they will remain as a memorial of the past and an encouragement for the future. In many a church and abbey in the old world hang the moldering relics of bygone years and our young nation now treasures up her memorials of these contests none the less brave.

The Iowa of 1860 with her 674,913 people has now become a commonwealth of 2,000,000 souls. In our prairie state are nearly half as many English-speaking people as trod the planet in the days of Shakespeare. Our state is young, but the possibilities of her future fill our hearts with hope and worthy pride. No blood or treasure has been spared to build and cement Iowa, the beautiful, as a part of the great temple of national unity. We have no anticipation of her future that we do not merge into that greater glory, the sisterhood of all the states. To-day closes a chapter of the record of the war. We deposit these silent yet eloquent memorials forever in the capitol. To the governor of our commonwealth we deliver them for the sacred keeping of coming generations, of a grateful, an honest, a patriotic and a Christian people. And now, as we lift our hearts in silent gratitude to Almighty God, let us one and all say, "God bless, God bless Old Glory forever."

...Group Five...

GOV. FRANK D. JACKSON

On Accepting the Flags in Behalf of the State.

VETERAN heroes of Iowa: We are all proud of the great achievements accomplished by the state of Iowa during her half century of existence, but let me assure you, my veteran friends, that in the minds and hearts of this great and intelligent people of Iowa, it all dwindles into insignificance beside the mighty heart-swelling of glory and pride which every loyal citizen of Iowa takes in the glorious record of deeds of valor of that gallant young army, which over thirty years ago she sent forth under the bright folds of these now tattered and faded battle flags.

The guns of Fort Sumter had hardly died away before an outraged people resolved to resent the insult made and to save the union. How well do I remember the stirring scenes that followed in the echoes of that fatal shot. The very air was charged with the spirit of patriotism. The fife and drum furnished the inspiration of liberty, while millions of loyal citizens kept step to the music of the union. Great war meetings were held in every community and crowded the largest halls to overflowing. Our cities and towns were thronged with a loyal and liberty-loving people. From the farms and workshops, from the counters and from the offices came the thousands ready to sacrifice their all for the glory and perpetuity of their country. I can hear those glorious songs of liberty now. I can hear the burning words of patriotism. I can see the thousands of young men in those great war meetings pushing their way down through the excited crowds, and amid storms of enthusiasm march out under the folds of their country's flag and sign the enlistment rolls to go forth to battle for their country's honor and the nation's life.

You, my brave friends, remember it all. You were all there. You remember how a few days later the company assembled in the public square to be mustered in. Everybody was there for miles around to see the boys march away. The fathers and mothers were there. The sisters and brothers, and sweethearts were all there. And amidst the cheers and tears, the sobs and heart-breakings, that gallant young company wheeled into line, keeping step to the roll of the beating drum and under the bright folds of these faded and tattered flags here to-day, marched away to battle and to die.

Four long and weary years the loyal hearts at home waited and prayed. With what earnestness did they scan the papers for the latest news from the front, and when the news came of another great battle, with what breathless eagerness did their eyes follow down the long list of dead and wounded to see if some of their own loved ones had fallen. How the hearts throbbed with joy over the news of a battle won. How they sank in anguish and despair at the information of defeat and death. And, finally, what joy and happiness fills the land when news is received that rebellion is crushed, that the flag of our country is saved; that the boys are coming home again. And how they waited and hoped and prayed for the return of those boys.

And here they come up the street keeping step to the roll of the same old drum; under the folds of the same old flag, now riddled and rent with shot and shell and stained with dust and blood. and yet a flag redeemed and saved to float forever over one country and a united people. Everybody was there with outstretched arms to welcome the boys back again. The old fathers and mothers were all there. And what a welcome! And with it all what sadness and anguish!

The company wheels into line to be mustered out. Here and there are vacant places of those who never returned. Here and there are those with one leg or one arm; others sick and emaciated, just from the hells of Andersonville and Libby.

Veteran soldiers of Iowa, let me assure you that from the beginning to the end of that mighty struggle the great loyal heart of Iowa was always with you and for you. It was with you just thirty-three years ago to-day when the rebel forces at Wilson's Creek formed ten different times and with glistening bayonets charged and recharged over the ground strewn with Iowa's dead and wounded, and ten times were hurled back to death and defeat by an Iowa regiment which stood there like a wall of adamant. How the great heart of Iowa throbbed and swelled with joy and pride over this first heroic defense of the honor of our state and the glory of our flag.

The heart of Iowa was with you at Shiloh, where Iowa soldiers fought with a heroism that is nursed only in the cradle of liberty, a heroism and bravery never surpassed in all the war history of the world.

It was with you at Donelson, where the flag of an Iowa regiment waves in everlasting glory and honor. The heart of Iowa was with you at Belmont and Pea Ridge, at Corinth and Prairie Grove, at Missionary Ridge and Atlanta. It was with you as you laid there in the trenches before Vicksburg. Every heart-throb of the great, loyal people of Iowa vibrated down into the very center of rebeldom, giving encouragement and cheer to the boys from Iowa. That great heart is still with you, veteran heroes of Iowa—only it is a bigger and a stronger heart. It's the heart of more than two millions of people, extending to you here to-day God's blessings along with its lasting love, its gratitude and its honor.

What a pleasure it would be for me here to-day, had I the time, to rehearse the glorious deeds of valor of Iowa regiments and Iowa soldiers. My first thought was to select some of the principal engagements during the war in which the Iowa troops participated, but after a careful investigation of the conspicuous part Iowa troops took in nearly all the great battles of the rebellion, I can tell you frankly that my task would be much shorter and lighter were I to relate to you that part of the war's history in which Iowa troops were not participants. Out of a population of a little over six hundred thousand, the young state of Iowa sent forth over seventy thousand to the defense of the flag. "It was Iowa soldiers that marched from the Des Moines river to the Atlantic ocean, and penetrated the interior of every rebel state in the union. It was an Iowa regiment that marched into South Carolina, tore down the rebel flag from her capitol, hoisted the stars and stripes, and brought the treasonable trophy back to Iowa, and it is here to-day, the property of our state."

In the language of a gallant Iowa soldier, from the beginning until the end the story of Iowa valor was the same as that

of tried comrades from other states.   Not greater, for all were
brave: but the Iowa soldiers were conspicuously so.   Their
fortune kept them at the front; they were the first everywhere.
These tattered and precious battle flags floated at the front in
every battle and were always found where tne conflict was the
thickest and the danger greatest.   At Wilson's Creek, Iuka,
Donelson and Shiloh, at Vicksburg, Atlanta, Allatoona, Chattanooga and Mobile, wherever Grant and Sherman led they followed, and to victory.   They were the heroes, the history
makers of the state; their deeds will live on forever.   From the
beginning to the end these scarred and tattered flags floated
over as brave an army as ever trod the face of the earth; over
a hundred battle fields they waved in triumph.

Ours was a war for freedom: a war for the unchaining of
millions of human beings.   Fortunate the people to whom is
given such a glorious opportunity to strike a blow for human
liberty.   And this is the record of but one young and vigorous
state in behalf of freedom.

Increase these 135 battle flags by those furnished by other
loyal states of this union, until they reach into the thousands,
and then merge them all into one great and glorious flag of
liberty: increase the awful sacrifice of human life until the
blood of a million men has been freely poured upon the altar of
our civil liberty, add to this a treasure of more than two billion
of dollars, and then you have only the tangible sacrifices made
by the loyal people of this great union in behalf of liberty.

What is this great flag of ours for which so much blood and
treasure has been spent?   It is the emblem representing the
will of sixty millions of American freemen, the uncrowned king
of this great republic.   I saw a regiment of soldiers a few days
ago assemble for parade.   I saw, as a distinction of honor, a
company selected to escort the colors to the parade grounds
and present them to the regiment, to the music of "The Star
Spangled Banner."   I saw the flag escorted between two
platoons of soldiers in front of the line and received at "present
arms" by the entire regiment—the highest honor that is given
in military tactics.

That flag is the uncrowned king of the American army.   In
line of review, when passing before the president of the United
States or the chief executive of the state, the flag is received
with greater honor and distinction than is accorded any human
being on the face of this earth.   With uncovered heads it is

received, because it stands for the majesty of law and for the will of the people. Surely that flag is the uncrowned king of the American people.

The flag of governments other than republics may represent the will of some of the people, but invariably there is a personality along with it represented in the arbitrary will of the ruler. Thank God the stars and stripes has no personality in it. It represents only the will of all the people. The chief executive, who is selected temporarily to administr and enforce the law, has no more personality in our flag than has the humblest citizen who stands beneath its protective folds. It is therefore a matter of surprise and regret that after more than a hundred years of national existence there are still citizens of this republic who fail to comprehend the relations of the citizen to the flag. It would seem as if the prejudice of centuries against the personality of the flag in despotic forms of government still exists here in America, and exists, too, against a flag that has no personality whatever. The stars and stripes stand for law, and that law made by the people, and in the making of that law every voter in this great land has had an exact and equal opportunity. How foolish it is then for American citizens to hurl personal epithets against the chief executive of the nation or state who is temporarily charged with the duty of maintaining the honor of the flag by enforcing the law which the people themselves have made. A wanton violation of law, whether by one person or a thousand, is not an insult to the executive of a state or nation, but an insult to the people themselves who made the law. And that insult is no greater so far as defying the will of the people and insulting the majesty of their law, in the commission of the crime of murder, than it is in the commission of a simple breach of the peace. The will of the people has been insulted, the majesty of law defied the flag spurned and humiliated, as much in the one case as in the other. Violation of law has been fixed by the will of the people as the starting point for putting the machinery in motion for the enforcement of law. Not a violation resulting in bloodshed, not a violation that destroys millions of property, but violation of law. No discretionary power is given the executive to wait for bloodshed or destruction of property before the machinery for enforcement shall be used. The commencement of violation is the signal for starting in motion the machinery for its enforcement.

Unfortunate it is for the American people that there seems to be a sentiment among some of them in direct opposition to their own laws; a sentiment demanding the executive to wait until somebody is killed or some vast amount of property destroyed before the enforcement of law begins. Study and reflection on behalf of these people, I am convinced, will result in the gradual advancement of this unwise public sentiment in some localities, up to those very wise laws, which these same people have made, which require the executive to commence the enforcement of the law at the instant law is violated. The insult to the flag and the people's law is no greater, made by the red handed anarchists in placing the torch where it destroys life and property, than it is by the so-called industrial army traveling through the country intimidating and holding up communities for food and shelter. Both are violations of law, both wanton insults to the people who made the law. A public sentiment which shall demand a rigid enforcement of all law by the executive of the nation, of states and of counties, is essential to the progress and perpetuity of our American government. A public sentiment which fails to demand the same swift and rigid enforcement of law against a thousand violators that it does against a single individual is a sickly sentiment indicative of governmental weakness, a maudlin sentimentality, dangerous alike to the freedom, happiness, and prosperity of the people. I am convinced that the strong and healthy sentiment of the American people demands that all the laws shall be obeyed, and that they shall be rigidly enforced whether it be against a single violator or a mob of ten thousand.

The blood and treasure expended to preserve this mighty fabric of civil liberty, is too awful a sacrifice to have it endangered now by a weak and sickly sentiment. A government, the best ever devised by mankind for the protection of the people's liberty, a government which gives the poor man better opportunities for advancement in life than any other government known to civilization, must not and will not be endangered and its usefulness impaired by the failure of a small portion of the American people to discern the difference between liberty in its broadest sense and license. Patriotism and loyalty in the enforcement of all law by the American people means the continual and lasting glory of the American republic.

Like an echo of the past come the words of inspiration from the immortal Lincoln: "Let reverence of law be breathed by every mother to the lisping babe that prattles on her lap; let it be taught in the schools, seminaries and colleges; let it be written in primers, spelling-books and almanacs; let it be preached from pulpits and proclaimed in legislative halls, and enforced in courts of justice. In short let it become the political re igion of the American people."

These loved and honored battle flags—how dear they are to the heart of Iowa. Once so bright and beautiful, now so ragged and tattered and faded. But we love them revere them and honor them for what they are and for all they represent. We love them because that grand old patriot, Iowa's war governor, sent you forth under the folds of these bright flags to battle and to die for liberty. We love them because their bright stars caught the last dying look of Iowa heroes on the field of glory. We love them with all their rags and tatters, because they are stained with the blood of Iowa's noblest, bravest and best. We love them because they waved in triumph over a hundred battle fields and because they always stood for liberty and for right.

In again assuming the care and protection of these precious emblems of liberty, let me assure you, veteran heroes, that the state of Iowa fully realizes and appreciates their priceless value. Here in Iowa's beautiful capitol they shall remain forever, forming a sacred altar around which will gather, in loving remembrance, the grateful hearts of more than two millions of people. As long as their faded folds shall hang together they shall teach the generations that are to follow, the loyalty and bravery of Iowa's soldiers. And when the hand of time shall have brushed away the last faded shred of these precious and priceless emblems, their memory shall remain forever an inspiration to deeds of honor, of heroism and of glory.

List and Description of

....Iowa Battle Flags....

Deposited in the Capitol Building
August 10, 1894.

LIST AND DESCRIPTION OF IOWA BATTLE FLAGS.

No. 1. National flag, First infantry: inscribed: "Springfield." Turned over by state historical society, August, 1894.

No. 2. National flag, Second infantry: inscribed: "2nd Regt. Iowa Vols." Official report of battle at Ft. Donelson by Colonel Tuttle, says: I cannot omit in this report an account of the color guard. Color Sergeant Doolittle fell early in the engagement, pierced by four balls and dangerously wounded. The colors were then taken by Corporal Page, Company B, who soon fell dead. They were again raised by Corporal Churcher, Company I, who had his arm broken just as he entered the entrenchments, when they were taken by Corporal Twombly, Company F, who was almost instantly knocked down by a spent ball, but immediately rose and bore them gallantly to the end of the fight. Not a single man of the color guard but himself was on his feet at the close of the engagement.

No. 3. National flag, Second infantry: inscribed: "Fort Donelson, Shiloh and Corinth."

No. 4. National flag, Second infantry.

No. 5. National flag, Second infantry; inscribed: "Fort Donelson."

No. 6. Banner, Second infantry.

No. 7. Banner, Second infantry.

No. 8. National flag, Third infantry; inscribed: "Blue Mills, Shiloh," "Siege of Corinth, Matamora," "Siege of Vicksburg, Jackson." This flag was captured before Atlanta, July 22, 1864, by Cleburne's division, and presented by Cleburne to Miss Laura J. Massengale (now Mrs. Pickett) who returned the flag to the adjutant-general of Iowa, August 7, 1883.

No. 9. National flag, Third infantry: inscribed: "Blue Mills, Shiloh, Siege of Corinth. Matamora, Vicksburg, Jackson, Atlanta, Sherman's March to the Sea, Savannah, the Carolinas."

No. 10. National flag, Fourth infantry: inscribed: "Pea Ridge, March 7 and 8, 1862."

No. 11. Banner, Fourth infantry.

No. 12. Banner, Fourth infantry.

No. 13. National flag, Fifth infantry.

No. 14. Banner, Fifth infantry: inscribed: "5th Regt. Iowa Vet. Vol. Infantry."

No. 15. Banner, Fifth infantry.

No. 16. Banner, Sixth infantry: inscribed: "6th Regt. Iowa Veteran Vols."

No. 17. National flag, Sixth infantry.

No. 18. National flag, Sixth infantry.

No. 19. National flag, Seventh infantry.

No. 20. National flag, Seventh infantry.

No. 21. Banner, Seventh infantry.

No. 22. Banner, Eighth infantry; inscribed: "8th Iowa Veteran Regt. Infantry."

No. 23. National flag, Eighth infantry.

No. 24. National flag, Eighth infantry: from the citizens of Memphis, July, 1864.

No. 25. Banner, Eighth infantry.

No. 26. Banner, Ninth infantry.

No. 27. Banner, Ninth infantry; received from sanitary fair of Dubuque, 1864, and presented to the adjutant-general September, 1889

No. 28. National flag, Ninth infantry; extract from history of regiment: "On the 22d of May (1863) in line with the whole army of the Tennessee, the regiment went first up to the assault. Its colors went down a few feet from the rebel works after the last one of its guard had fallen, either killed or wounded, and its dripping folds were drawn thence from under the bleeding body of its prostrate bearer."

No. 29. National flag, Ninth infantry: inscriptions: "Pea Ridge, Chickasaw Bayou Arkansas Post, Jackson,

Siege of Vicksburg, Cherokee, Tuscumbia, Lookout Mountain, Missionary Ridge, Ringgold, Resaca, Dallas, New Hope, Big Shanty, Kenesaw Mountain, Chattahoochie, Atlanta, Jonesboro, Lovejoy and Eden Station, Savannah, Congaree Creek, Columbia, Bentonville."

No. 30. Banner, Tenth infantry; inscribed: "Tenth Iowa Veterans."

No. 31. Banner, Tenth infantry; inscribed: "10th Iowa Veteran Vols."

No. 32. National flag, Eleventh infantry.

No. 33. National flag, Eleventh infantry.

No. 34. Banner, Eleventh infantry.

No. 35. Banner, Twelfth infantry; inscribed: "Our liberties we prize and our rights we will maintain."

No. 36. Banner, Twelfth infantry; inscribed: "12th Iowa Veteran Vol. infantry."

No. 37. National flag, Twelfth infantry; inscribed: "Fort Donelson, Shiloh, Corinth."

No. 38. National flag, Thirteenth infantry; inscribed: "Siege of Corinth, Iuka, Corinth, Vicksburg, Atlanta, Savannah, Columbia, Bentonville, Raleigh." The first United States flag raised over the state house at Columbia, S. C., by Lieut.-Col. J C. Kennedy, Thirteenth Iowa Veteran Volunteer infantry, February 17, 1865.

No. 39. National flag, Fourteenth infantry; inscribed: "Donelson, Shiloh, Corinth."

No. 40. Banner, Fourteenth infantry; turned over to adjutant-general, under authority from war department dated December 6, 1864, by adjutant Fourteenth infantry.

No. 41. National flag, Fifteenth infantry; inscribed: "Corinth;" turned over to adjutant-general by L. S. Tyler, 1891.

No. 42. National flag, Fifteenth infantry; from L. S. Tyler, 1891.

No. 43. National flag, Fifteenth infantry; inscribed: "Shiloh, Siege of Corinth, Iuka, Corinth, Nicka Jack, July 4th, 5th and 7th, 1864. Vicksburg, Atlanta, July 21st, 22nd, and 28th, 1864. Mediden, Atlanta and Savannah."

No. 44. National flag, Fifteenth infantry; inscribed: "Siege of Corinth, Corinth, Vicksburg, Monroe, Meriden, Bolton's Cross Roads, Big Shanty, Kenesaw, Nicka Jack, Chattahoochie, Before Atlanta July 20, 21, 22, and 28. Jonesboro, Lovejoy's Station, Atlanta, Snake Creek Gap, Savannah, Pocotaligo, Salkehatchie, Orangebury, Columbia, Fayetteville, Bentonville, Goldsboro, N. C."

No. 45. Banner, Fifteenth infantry; inscribed: "15th Iowa Veteran Vols."

No. 46. Banner, Fifteenth infantry; from L. S. Tyler, 1891.

No. 47. Banner, Fifteenth infantry.

No. 48. National flag, Sixteenth infantry; captured with the regiment July 22, 1864, before Atlanta; returned to regiment during reunion in 1883 by General Govan and turned over to adjutant-general by Col. A. H. Saunders in 1884.

No. 49. National flag, Sixteenth infantry.

No. 50. Banner, Sixteenth infantry.

No. 51. Banner, Sixteenth infantry.

No. 52. National flag, Seventeenth infantry.

No. 53. National flag, Seventeenth infantry; turned over by Col. D. B. Hillis in 1883.

No. 54. National flag, Seventeenth infantry; inscribed: "Siege of Corinth, May 28, 1862; Iuka, September 19, 1862; Corinth, October 3 and 4, 1862; Raymond, May 12, 1863; Jackson. May 14, 1863; Champion Hills, May 16, 1863; Siege of Vicksburg. May 22, 1863; Fort Hill, July 26, 1863; Mission Ridge, November 25, 1863; Atlanta, July 27 and 28, 1864; Tilton, October 13, 1864; Savannah, December 21, 1864; Columbia, February 17, 1865; Bentonville, March 18-22, 1865."

No. 55. Banner, Seventeenth infantry

No. 56. Banner, Seventeenth infantry.

No. 57. Banner, Eighteenth infantry.

No. 58. Banner, Eighteenth infantry.

No. 59. National flag, Eighteenth infantry.

No. 60. Banner, Nineteenth infantry.

No. 61. National flag, Nineteenth infantry; "Prairie Grove, Ark., Dec. 7th, 1862; Van Buren. Ark , Dec. 28, 1862; Vicksburg, Miss., July 4, 1863; Yazoo, Miss.,

July 13, 1863: Sterling Farm, La., Sept. 29, 1863;
Brownsville, Texas, Nov. 6, 1863."

No. 62.   National flag, Nineteenth infantry; inscribed: "Prairie
Grove, Ark., Dec. 7, 1862; Van Buren, Ark., Dec.
28, 1862: Vicksburg, Miss., July 4, 1863; Yazoo
City, Miss., July 13, 1863: Sterling Farm, Sept.
29, 1863; Brownsville, Texas, Nov. 6, 1863."

No. 63.   National flag, Twentieth infantry.

No. 64.   Banner, Twentieth infantry.

No. 65.   Banner, Twentieth infantry.

No. 66.   National flag, Twenty-first infantry.

No. 67.   Banner, Twenty-first infantry; inscribed: "Port Gibson, Champion Hills, Black River Bridge, Hunts-
ville, Vicksburg, Jackson."

No. 68.   Banner, Twenty-second infantry.

No. 69.   Banner, Twenty-second infantry. Received from war
department, 1894, through Hon. J H. Gear.

No. 70.   National flag, Twenty-second infantry. Received from
J. C. Schrader, August, 1894.

No. 71.   Banner, Twenty-third infantry.

No. 72.   National flag, Twenty-third infantry; inscribed: "Port
Gibson. May 1st, 1863: Champion Hills, May 16,
1863: Black River Bridge, May 17, 1863: Millikens
Bend, June 7, 1863: Vicksburg, May, 18th to 22nd,
Vicksburg, July 4, 1863: Jackson, July 9th to 16th,
1863: Fort Esperanza, November 27 and 28, 1863."

No. 73.   National flag, Twenty-fourth infantry; inscribed:
"Port Gibson, Champion Hills, Jackson, Sabine
Cross Roads. Opegan, Fishers Hill, Cedar Creek."

No. 74.   National flag, Twenty-fifth infantry.

No. 75.   National flag, Twenty-fifth infantry.

No. 76.   Banner flag, Twenty-fifth infantry.

No. 77.   Banner, Twenty-fifth infantry.

No. 78.   Banner, Twenty-fifth infantry.

No. 79.   Banner, Twenty-sixth infantry.

No. 80.   National flag, Twenty-sixth infantry.

No. 81.   National flag, Twenty-sixth infantry.

No. 82.   National flag, Twenty-seventh infantry; inscribed:
"Little Rock, Sept. 10, 1863: Ft. De Russey, La.,
May 18, 1864; Ditch Bayou, Ark., July 6, 1864:
Tupelo, Miss., July 14, 1864; Old Town Creek, July

15, 1864: Nashville, Dec. 15, 1864; Siege and Capture of Blakely, April 2 to 9, 1865."

No. 83. Banner, Twenty-seventh infantry.

No. 84. Banner, Twenty-seventh infantry.

No. 85. National flag, Twenty-eighth infantry: inscribed: "Port Gibson, Edwards Station, Champion Hills, Vicksburg, Jackson."

No. 86. Banner Twenty-eighth infantry.

No. 87. Banner, Twenty-eighth infantry.

No. 88. National flag. Twenty-eighth infantry: inscribed: "Port Gibson Edwards Station Champion Hills, Vicksburg, Jackson Sabine Cross Roads, Cane River, Middle Bayou, Mansura, Yellow Bayou, Opequan, Fishers Hill, Cedar Creek."

No. 89. Banner, Twenty-ninth infantry. Turned over by Col. Thomas H. Benton, Jr., August 25, 1865.

No. 90. National flag, Thirtieth infantry. Turned over by Col. A. Roberts. June 17, 1865.

No. 91. National flag, Thirtieth infantry: inscribed: "Battles participated in by the 30th Regt Iowa Vol. Infantry, Chickasaw Bayou, Arkansas Post, Battle of 19th and 22d of May and Siege of Vicksburg. Jackson, Brandon, Cherokee Station, Lookout Mountain, Missionary Ridge, Ringgold, Resaca, Dallas, Kenesaw Mountain, Nicka Jack, Before Atlanta July 22nd to 28th, Jonesboro, Lovejoy's Station, Bentonville, and Raleigh."

No. 92. National flag, Thirty-first infantry.

No. 93. Banner, Thirty-first infantry.

No. 94. Banner, Thirty-first infantry.

No. 95. National flag, Thirty-first infantry. Chickasaw Bayou, Arkansas Post, Fourteen Mile Creek, Vicksburg assaults 19th and 22d of May, Jackson, Canton, Cherokee Station, Tuscumbia, Lookout Mountain, Mission Ridge, Ringgold, Resaca, Dallas, New Hope Church, Kenesaw Mountain, Chattahoochie River, Decatur, Atlanta, Jonesboro, Lovejoy, Little River, Savannah, Congaree Creek, Columbia, Bentonville and Raleigh.

No. 96. National flag, Thirty-second infantry: Cape Girardeau, Bayou Metaire, Fort De Russey, Pleasant Hills, Marksville, Yellow Bayou, Lake Chicot, Tupelo,

Old Town Creek, Nashville, Brentwood Hills, Ft Blakely; from the ladies of Waterloo, 1864.

No. 97. Banner, Thirty-third infantry.

No. 98. National flag, Thirty-third infantry; Yazoo Pass, Helena, Little Rock, Prairie D'Ann, Poison Springs, Jenkins' Ferry, Mobile.

No. 99. Banner, Thirty-fourth infantry.

No. 100. National flag, Thirty-fourth infantry: Chickasaw Bluff, Arkansas Post Vicksburg, Yazoo City, Ft. Esperanza.

No. 101. National flag, Thirty-fourth infantry.

No. 102. Banner, Thirty-fifth infantry.

No. 103. Banner, Thirty-fifth infantry.

No. 104. National flag, Thirty-fifth infantry

No. 105. National flag. Thirty-fifth infantry.

No. 106. Banner, Thirty-sixth infantry.

No. 107. Banner, Thirty-sixth infantry.

No. 108. National flag, Thirty-eighth infantry; turned over to adjutant-general by Robert McNutt, late surgeon of regiment, in 1888.

No. 109. National flag, thirty-ninth infantry: Parker's Cross Roads, Tenn., 1862; Cherokee Station, Ala., 1863; Town Creek, Ala., 1863; Snake Creek Gap, Ga., 1864; Lay's Ferry, Ga., 1864; Allatoona, Ga., 1864; Columbia, S. C., 1865; Bentonville, N. C., 1865.

No. 110. National flag, Thirty-ninth infantry; turned over by Col. J. M. Griffith, August, 1894.

No. 111. Banner, Thirty-ninth infantry; turned over by Col. J. M. Griffith, August, 1894.

No. 112. National flag, Fortieth infantry; Helena, Little Rock, Elkin's Ford, Prairie D'Ann, Camden, Jenkins' Ferry, Marks' Mills Fort Pemberton.

No. 113. National flag, First colored regiment, infantry (also known as Sixtieth U. S. colored infantry).

No. 114. Banner, unknown; received from adjutant-general of Wisconsin.

No. 115. Banner, First battery: first at Pea Ridge, March 7 and 8, 1862; Lookout Mountain, Kenesaw Mountain; Atlanta, July 20, 21, 22 and 28th; first at Port Gibson, May 1, 1863; Atlanta, August 11, 1864; Missionary Ridge, Resaca, Dallas, New

Hope, Church. Chickasaw, Arkansas Post, Siege
of Vicksburg, Chattahoochie River, Jackson,
Cherokee, Tuscumbia: presented by the city of
Burlington to First Iowa battery, February 15,
1864.

No. 116. Banner, First Iowa battery. "First at Pea Ridge,
March 7th and 8th, 1862; Chickasaw Bayou, Arkan-
sas Post, Port Gibson, Jackson, Siege of Vicks-
burg, Cherokee, Tuscumbia, Lookout Mountain,
Resaca, Dallas, Burnt Hickory, Kenesaw, Nicka
Jack, Atlanta, Jonesboro, Lovejoy Station."

No. 117. National flag, Second battery.

No. 118. National flag, Second battery. (Veteran.)

No. 119. Banner, Third battery; "Sugar Creek, February 17th,
Pea Ridge, March 7th and 8th; Helena, July 4th;
Ft. Pemberton; Little Rock." Presented to battery in fall of 1862 by ladies of Milwaukee. The
coat of arms of Iowa is placed on one side and
that of Wisconsin on the other.

No. 120. National flag, First cavalry.

No. 121. Banner (small), Second cavalry. (Veteran.)

No. 122. Banner (small), Second cavalry. (Veteran.)

No. 123. Guidon, Second cavalry.

No. 124. Guidon, Second cavalry.

No. 125. Guidon, Third cavalry.

No. 126. Banner (small), Third cavalry.

No. 127. National flag, Third cavalry.

No. 128. National flag, Third cavalry. (Veteran.) "Pea Ridge,
Kirksville, Vicksburg, Little Rock, Harrisburg,
Big Blue, Osage, Montevallo, Ala., Mch. 31, 1865;
Ebenezer Church, April 1, 1865; Columbus, Ga.,
April 16, 1865; Selma, Ala., April 2, 1865."

No. 129. Guidon, Fourth cavalry.

No. 130. Banner (small), Fourth cavalry.

No. 131. National flag, Fourth cavalry. Big Blue, October 23,
1864; Osage, October 25, 1864; Jackson, May 14,
July 9 to July 14, 1863, February 5, 1864; Haines
Bluff—captured by Fourth Iowa cavalry, May 19,
1863; Siege of Vicksburg, 1863; Canton, July, 1863;
Medidian, February 4, 1864; Tupelo, July 13, 1864;
Selma, April 2, 1865, and closing battles.

No. 132. Banner (small), Fifth cavalry.   (Veteran.)
No. 133. Banner (small), Fifth cavalry.
No. 134. Banner, Seventh cavalry.
No. 135. Guidon, Eighth cavalry.
No. 136. Banner, Eighth cavalry.
No. 137. Guidon, Eighth cavalry.
No. 138. National flag, Thirty-fifth infantry. Jackson, May
14; Vicksburg; Jackson, July 16; Henderson Hill;
Pleasant Hill; Mansuri; Yellow Bayou; Old River
Lake; Tupelo.

www.ingramcontent.com/pod-product-compliance
Lightning Source LLC
Chambersburg PA
CBHW020315090426
42735CB00009B/1353